Build Email List from Scratch with These 100+ Email Marketing Tips and Enhance Your Email Campaign (Use Email Marketing Best Practices To Increase Web Traffic.)

GlobeWorld Publication

Part 1

How to Gather Email Addresses

Wrong or inadequate information about email marketing could get most of the messages you send out in the spam folder instead of the inbox. With so many online marketers around, many people's emails are full of content and you have to be extra smart to ensure that you stand out and all your messages end up in the inbox. However, having many subscribers might be of no use to you if they do not convert into customers. Nonetheless, with all the hype about the best email marketing methods to use going on in the internet, it is possible to get all the basics wrong. This guide is here to show you how you can build an email list from scratch, increase the success rate of your email marketing campaigns, and see your business grow.

Although building an email list can be daunting, you could achieve much success if you are patient. You should consider hiring the services of email marketing experts to guide you along the way, in case you feel you need help. Nevertheless, in case you are confident of your ability, then go for it. Having a long list of email subscribers could give you peace of mind, since you will have the means to reach customers any time you launch a new product or want to sell existing products. It is also a good way to launch into affiliate marketing, whereby you can sell other people's products to your audience and make some profit. You will no longer need to depend on PPC, CPM, CPC, CPA and such other methods get customers, but you will have a large database of customers any time you need them. Thanks to the internet, many successful marketers have used email marketing to explode their business and put bread on the table.

Nevertheless, before you start your email marketing campaign; it is important to know your target audience. Once you do that, is it is time to gather their email information, in case you do not have it. You can follow the following guidelines to make your email gathering task a success.

1) **Have a goal.**
   It is important that you have a goal before you start gathering email addresses; otherwise, you will burn yourself out before you know it. A clear goal will motivate you to keep going even when the email-address gathering task seems formidable.

2) **Define your audience.**
   Determining the sort of audience you want to reach out before you start your email campaign is important too. This can give you an idea on the sort of messages to draft when reaching out to them. Moreover, this would enable you to get an audience that is relevant and can easily convert.

3) **Build an audience.**

Build an audience through your blog, social media, website, or any other platform where users engage with your brand.

4) Use incentives to encourage sign up

People like to get incentives before they can sign up. Give them that. Show them how they will benefit by signing up to your email list. Come up with innovative incentives that would encourage them to sign up, such as giving them a special offer on a rare commodity or service. You can check out what special offers your competitors are giving and offer better ones to leverage the game.

5) Make it easy to subscribe.

Make it easy for people to subscribe to your email list. Preferably, put the option for that at the top and right hand corner of your blog or web page. Make the option visible, and avoid arm-twisting people by asking them to sign up before they view the content on your blog or web page, since this could be counterproductive.

6) Get contact information by promising newsletter, seminar, or free training.

You can get the contact information on your target audience by promising them newsletters, free seminar, guides, more information about your products and services, free training, or even free software. The best way to do this is to have an obvious button on your web page or blog that enables your readers to sign up when they visit the page.

7) Use double opt-in forms to capture new subscribers.

People who sign up through double opt-in forms are more likely to appreciate your correspondence than those who you send direct email or those who you gather using single opt-in. This is because they have to confirm by clicking a link in an email that you send them requesting them to verify that they actually signed up to your service and will appreciate further correspondence from you.

8) Avoid asking annoying questions when gathering contact information.

Asking your readers annoying questions when gathering their contact information could affect your email gathering efforts negatively. Make sure you ask only for relevant and important information. Keep an accurate data of all the information they have given you to avoid asking them the same questions again.

9) Reach out for customers wherever they are.

With the world evolving, so fast, consumers want to connect with businesses through a variety of ways. Do not be afraid to reach new consumers through social media, online ads and whatever means at your disposal. You can even grow your email list by placing a guest book or a sign up form in your business and asking your customers to go to your Facebook page or website and sign up.

Email Marketing Best Practices

Once you have gathered your email list, it is time to start your email marketing campaign. Good management of your email list will make your work easier and enjoyable. You can follow the tips below to make your campaign more effective.

1) **Segment your subscribers.**

   Segment your audience by their demographics, interests or preference, to make your email campaign more manageable. That way, you will know which content fits your subscribers and send the right content to the right people.

2) **Avoid automation of greetings and welcome message.**

   Take your time, draft your greetings and welcome message so that they seem personal. Automating greetings and welcome messages can be counterproductive, since that gives the impression that you are not familiar with your subscribers. Refer to them by name, but do not overdo this, to avoid looking creepy.

3) **Use polls to get opinions on a single topic.**

   Creating an opinion poll about an interesting topic can be exciting to customers, especially when they have to vote for something they hold dear. It gets more exciting when they see how others have responded to the same questions in the opinion poll. This can foster a sense of interaction.

4) **Avoid generic messages.**

   Avoid sending out single generic messages since your readers have varying interests and tastes. Segment your readers, according to their interests, preferences, demographics, etc. and send the messages that you think are relevant to each group. This will ensure that only those who are interested in certain products get particular emails.

5) **Determine your content.**

   The content you send out should be well targeted. Be straightforward, and do not keep your readers guessing on what exactly you are trying to sell them. In case you are offering a free service or product such as a seminar or eBooks, say so explicitly, and state why you are doing that.

6) **Determine how often you should send an email.**

   The frequency at which you send emails is important. Determine how often you should do that before you start your email campaign. This will prevent you from mailing too frequently, since that could make your readers to relegate your emails to the spam folder. Make a sensible schedule and follow it.

7) **Be trustworthy.**

   Make sure that you deliver what you promise your audience. Do not promise what you cannot deliver with the hope that this will increase your email list. Many individuals fall into the trap of promising heaven on earth, but are unable to live up to their promises, thus triggering mass unsubscribes.

8) Be supportive.
Let your audiences know that you care about them. Some of your email subscribers might sign up for your service only to discover that this is not what they needed. In case they send you queries asking you to refer them to the best subscription, be supportive and do that.

9) Be useful.
Ensure you do not only talk about marketing and your services in your emails. Give your audiences contents that would add value to them. Nevertheless, avoid giving content that your audiences do not need, no matter how cool it might seem. That includes pornography, and religious teachings, unless they ask for it. You can find out what exactly your audiences need by asking them.

10) Avoid wasting people's time.
Time is money and many people are quite busy even to read an email. Once your audiences are ready to listen to you and start opening your emails, ensure that you are straight to the point and give them only relevant content.

11) Do not repeat people's names too much.
As much as you would like to believe that your email subscribers are your friends, the truth of the matter is that most of them are not your friends. Therefore, avoid making it so personal when communicating with them. Do not repeat their names too much in the email, lest you look sinister.

12) Reward people with tips, gossip, etc.
Nothing can be as boring as constantly receiving emails that are only laden with marketing information. Occasionally surprise your subscribers with useful tips. Give them tips about the latest trends in fashion, movies, politics, or in any other area where you are an expert, so that they can look forward to reading your emails. However, do not overdo it.

13) Be interesting.
Nothing can put off the audience more than boring emails. Spice up your content and be interesting. You do not have to write your emails like a suspense thriller, but you can give them an element of suspense, so that your audiences do not know what exactly to expect in your next email.

14) Be creative and innovative.
Do not be so formulaic when writing your emails. Occasionally tweak them up a bit, so that they do not always seem the same, lest your audience think that you are re-sending the same content. Better still, you should carefully monitor all the emails you send out, and then tweak them a bit when you notice that they have become too monotonous.

15) Do not swindle people.

Defrauding people is a no-no. Although it might seem the easiest way out, it can damage your reputation. In case you are unable to deliver, what you promised on time, alert your customers about it early enough and fulfill your promise the soonest. This is a good way to prove that you are a trustworthy person.

16) Use numbers and bullets in your email.

Numbers and bullets stop the eyes from wandering too much in an email. Use them to the maximum effect, so that even when your email is too long, your audiences will read quickly. It would also make them to grasp and digest your points easily and in a more natural way.

17) Be promising of something good.

Make sure your emails promise something good and interesting. Do not write dry emails, which make you appear as if all you want is to make some quick money. Let your audiences know that your offer would better their lives, and the sooner they take it the better.

18) Use Short text messages that can be printed or scanned.

Most people are busy and do not have the time, even to read emails, and would prefer to scan or print an interesting email when they get it. Make it easy for them to do that by using short text messages that they can easily scan or print. In other words, make sure your messages do not sound like a long sermon.

19) Ask questions.

Ask your audiences what they would like to hear from you and how they would like you to present your content. Their answers could give you an idea on which is the best way forward and enable you to tweak your messages appropriately. You do not have to ask all your audiences the same question, but you can segment them into groups, and post your questionnaire to them, one group at a time.

20) Be personal and tone down that business-like look.

For best results in your email marketing campaigns, be personal with your audiences. This will make them know that you are human and not a robot or a machine. Give them the impression that you identify with them. Once you have them by your side, you will discover that it would be easier to convert them from being an audience to customers.

21) Be natural.

Nothing can put off email subscribers than you sounding unnatural. Be yourself and let them know from the start that you have limitations, lest they put too much expectation on you, and demand what you cannot deliver. State clearly what you can deliver from the start and what you cannot. Do not give the impression that you can make your customers rich overnight, unless you can do that.

Part 2

How to Sell Using Email

Now that you have an email list and set things in motion, it is time you know how to sell using email. It is a fact that many people are selling through emails and your emails have to stand out so that they can make an impression on the reader. You can achieve this objective by doing the following things.

1) **Prepare people to buy before you start selling.**

   For best results, prepare new subscribers before you can start selling them any of your products. Do not rush, but ensure that they have started opening your emails, before offering them hard stuff. You can use the numerous tools and apps online to track the number of emails opened by your audiences.

2) **Practice by sending out test emails.**

   Practice by sending test emails before sending actual ones to see how they look in different email providers such as Yahoo, Gmail, Hotmail/MSN/Live or even Outlook client. Make any changes to the format of your emails in case you notice that they do not look okay in some email providers, and send them out again, until you are satisfied with the result.

3) **Ask friends and family about the best strategies to use.**

   In case you are new in email marketing, your friends and family can give you useful tips on how to go about building an email list. Ask questions and find out what sort of marketing emails they would like to receive and what puts them off. Note that down and use their advice when you start your email marketing campaign.

4) **Edit your emails.**

   Editors edit their content to perfection before publishing it. Therefore, edit your emails too before you send them out. Grammar and typo errors can put off potential customers. Remember, an error free email will enable your subscribers to read quickly and save time. This can make the difference on whether they will read your emails in the future or not.

5) **Send people what they want.**

   Find out what sort of messages people really like to receive before you start sending out emails. In case you are unable to find out what exactly they need, you can occasionally tweak your messages to see which version receives the most responses. Ensure that you do not send boring or irrelevant messages to your readers.

6) Show the advantages of your product.

Alert your customers of the advantages of having your product. Remember, they might have received similar messages in the past, and so, you need to show them that your product is not just another product, but it is something that can add value to them.

7) Insert numerous links, which are obvious.

Insert numerous links that lead to your landing page in your emails and make them obvious. Preferably, insert the first link within the first 100 pixels of your email and throughout the email. This would make it easier for your audiences to click them to find out what is on offer.

8) Minimize the use of images and use well-coded HTML instead.

A picture can say more than a thousand words, but minimize them in your emails. You have to remember that an email is not a web or print page. Many subscribers would view the email in the preview panel, which might make it difficult for them to see the pictures. Moreover, many mobile devices cannot display such pictures. Use well coded HTML instead, since it is more effective.

9) Put an unsubscribe button and make it visible.

Ensure that you make it easy for your audiences to unsubscribe when they need to do that. This means you should place the unsubscribe button where they can easily see it without having to scroll through a long email. Although this might seem counterproductive, it can prevent frustrated readers who are trying to unsubscribe from flagging your emails as spam.

10) Follow anti-spam rules to avoid your email being flagged and considered spam.

Ensure you have spam tips readily available to prevent the emails you send out ending up in the spam folder instead of your recipient's inbox. Failure to follow basic anti-spam rules could deny you a chance to get your emails into the inbox of your subscribers for a long time, even months or years.

11) Use appropriate email dimensions - not more than 500-650 pixels.

The usage of appropriate email dimensions is imperative. Using very large dimensions could make your recipients, especially those who read your emails through their mobile, to scroll horizontally so that they can view images. Use 500-650 pixels for best results.

12) Clean your email list and make it concise.

A cluttered email list can be counterproductive. Clean up your email list and make it concise. This would enable you to respond to your subscribers' orders and queries easily. Get rid of any email address that does not add value to your email marketing campaigns. However, ensure that you note down such emails somewhere, since you might need them in future.

13) Ask users to add you to their email list.

Ask your subscribers to add you to their email list. This is a good way to nurture a healthy relationship and encourage interaction. They might be people building an email list too, and would not mind adding you to their email list.

14) Use Text and Html based Messages.

No doubt, you want as many people as possible to open and read your messages.
Therefore, use both text and HTML based messages, which enables people to view your content even when they use their mobiles. Select the font that is readable in most browsers and devices. You can do this by experimenting with different fonts then sending them out to your own email address, to see how they appear on an ordinary phone.

15) Measure your performance.

It would be difficult for you to determine whether your email campaign is a success or not unless you regularly measure your performance. You can measure your performance by using tracking tools and trackable links, and keep a record of the same, so that you can know where you need some improvement. Moreover, measure the number of people who have signed up since your last email campaign, to get an idea on how you are performing. Too little sign ups should not send you into a panic, but should motivate you to be more effective in your email campaigns.

16) Measure clicks and unsubscribe rate.

No matter how effective you are in your email campaigns, you will discover that some of your audience will unsubscribe due to one reason or another. Measure unsubscribe rate to find out how many people are unsubscribing from your email list and why. Measure the click-through rate (CTR) regularly too.

17) Let links lead people to the landing page.

No matter how many links you insert in your email, it would be a waste of time if they do not lead your readers to your landing pages. Therefore, ensure the links you include in your emails lead people there. Most important, reserve most of the information your readers need to know about your product on the landing page. The email is only a bait to get them there to find out what exactly is on offer.

18) Make asking additional questions optional

When you need to ask for additional information from your readers, make that optional and explain why the information is necessary. In addition, instead of asking for street address, asking general questions such as the zip code are more effective. You will get most of the information you need later directly or indirectly from your readers, once they have signed up. Therefore, do not push too hard at first.

19) Encourage people to reply in a friendly way.

You will never know what people think of your emails unless they tell you. You can ask for their opinion by requesting them to reply in a friendly way. Remember, they are not obligated to reply, so take no offense in case they fail to do that.

20) Use your real name as "From" Address.

Since your aim is to get as close as possible to your email subscribers, you should use your real name as "From" Address. This will show that you are an honest person. That way, your readers will regard the emails you send as coming from a friend. Although you put your reputation at stake by using your real name as "from" address, that can earn you bonus points. Moreover, it can motivate you to be more honest when dealing with your subscribers.

21) Send only relevant text/content.

Only send content that is relevant and which can make your email campaign more effective. Your readers have plenty of places where they can read cheap gossip, jokes, and funny stuff, so minimize on that. Only include such content if you are convinced that it will improve the overall performance of your campaign. Moreover, avoid being a jack-of-all-trades by professing to offer all kinds of services.

22) Build an exclusive club.

Create an atmosphere of an exclusive club. That way, your target audience will feel special when they receive your email. Give them the impression that they are the selected few. Make them feel part of the family. Always refer to them in your media outlet such as a blog or a web page, so that they feel they belong.

23) Make people happy.

When possible, make people happy. Motivate and inspire them. Occasionally include an inspiring quote in your emails. Give the impression that it is not all about money, but you would like to forge a lifelong relationship with them. That way, they can easily open up and give you a feedback when you need to know how you are performing in your email marketing campaign.

24) Include downloads.

Including free downloads in your email can be quite effective. You can give your readers links where they can download software, movies, eBooks, and such stuff for free. That way, they will feel you add value to them, and will be more likely to open your emails when they see them, since they know they come with freebies.

25) Use social proof.

Most people like to know whether your product or service is worth their money before investing in it. Give them social proof that they are making a worthy investment by showing them reviews of people who have bought your products. Always include verified purchase reviews in your emails, since this can help fence sitters to make a decision.

26) Emphasize on Clear call-to-action.

Once you draft your emails, make sure you instruct your audiences what you want them to do. This would enable them know what you expect from them and thus respond accordingly. If you want them to buy a product, tell them so explicitly. Do not beat around the bush and make it seem as if you are offering freebies.

27) Give deadlines and show urgency.

Draft your messages in such a way that they have a sense of urgency. Make your audiences and customers know that time is limited and your offer will not last forever. Give them a deadline as to when you expect them to take your offer, or it will be gone forever. Show them that they stand to lose if they miss out within a particular time.

28) Say thank you.

With so many online marketers competing for the same customers, do not take your readers for granted. An average reader has subscribed to at least five email lists. At the far end are those who receive hundreds of emails every day. Therefore, show your readers that you appreciate their effort to open your email by telling them thank you.

29) Show that you care.

The best way to tame a person and get them closer is by showing that you care. Ensure that you show your subscribers that the emails you send are there to better their lives and not to fleece them. Do not give them threats or ultimatums that they should respond to your emails or you will unsubscribe them from your email list. Remember, they owe you nothing, and harassing them is the last thing you should do.

30) Ask for feedback.

Periodically ask your readers for feedback in a polite way. This will help you gauge exactly how many people are interested in your emails. You should consider stopping sending emails to some people when they stay too long without getting in touch with you. Surely, you do not want your emails to end up in the inbox of persons who died like ten years ago.

31) Be conversational.

Draft your messages in a conversational way. As you write your content, try to imagine that you are communicating with a real person. Therefore, talk to them in a friendly and a conversational way that would not only appeal to their intellect, but also their hearts and emotions. Do not be too formal; talk as you would talk to a friend.

32) Pique interest and keep readers on their toes.

Do not allow your subscribers to know what exactly is up your sleeves. Pique their interests by fashioning your messages in an interesting, suspenseful way. That way, even though they know that your product is not unique, they will want to learn more about it, and will keep opening and reading your emails.

33) Add referral codes to your emails.

Adding referral codes to your emails can help you reach more people. Encourage your readers to forward your messages and refer others to you. The good thing about this is that your audience will help you to spread the word around about your product without you spending a dime.

34) Use buttons to enable people to click.

Use buttons to enable people to click on the landing page. Do not tuck the buttons somewhere unreachable. The whole idea is to bring people to your landing page and not merely to have a long email list. Remember, the earlier you convince them to convert, the better for you, since you will recover any investment you have made in your email marketing campaign faster.

35) Remind readers what to do.

People forget quickly. Keep reminding your audience what to do next. However, do not bug them. Reminding them that you need them to click a certain link after every sentence can be a put off. Remind them twice in a short email and four to five times in a long email.

36) Tap into the current trend and events.

Occasionally give your subscribers an update into the current trends and events. You can give them an update on the latest movies, fashion, and job offers etc. Use brief words to do this and do not start your email with such stuff or put them in the subject line. Put them at the end of your email to encourage people to read your emails to the end.

37) Behave like a friend to get your emails opened.

Sending an email is not an end onto itself, but a means towards an end. You want people to open and read your emails. Therefore, encourage them to do that by being friendly. Moreover, do not send very long messages to people who just signed up. Reserve those for people who have been with you for a while. Send short, sweet messages to encourage new subscribers to open your emails.

38) Use powerful words.

Use powerful words in your emails. By that, I do not mean vocabularies, but words that are straight to the point and effective. Be bold when describing your product or services, since this shows that you are confident of what you are offering. No one can believe in your product or service if you do not show passion for it.

39) Use "You" when referring to your subscribers.

Refer to your readers with the "you" voice. This could make them pay more attention to what you have to say. Avoid using the word "we" with your readers. For instance, instead of saying, "We can make the world a better place by conserving energy." You should say, "You can make the world a better place by conserving energy."

40) Treat your audience like VIPs.

Treat your audience with courtesy and make them feel special. Your email list might contain all sorts of people, even the president, so you cannot underestimate the social standards of your readers. When they send you a query, you should answer them politely, and avoid repeating their names too much. Remember, they are not your golf friends, but potential customers.

41) Invest your time in the job.

Building an email list can be tedious and frustrating. Develop a tough skin and be prepared to invest your time in the task. Plan early in case you need to send out numerous emails. Avoid using the "send all mail" option in your Compose Email tab, since this would mean all your recipients would see who else have received the email. This could violate their privacy. Moreover, an unscrupulous subscriber could get a chance to scoop email addresses at random and use them for sinister motives.

42) Do research on the best email marketing practices from experts.

Learn tricks from people who have been doing email marketing for a while, especially those who are successful in their campaigns. You can subscribe to their email lists and see how they draft their content. Subscribe to their newsletter too, and learn as much as possible from them.

43) Be loyal to your audience and deliver what you promise.

Defrauding people is not ethical. Word spread fast and you could easily damage your reputation when word gets out that you are not an honest person. Always deliver what you promise and be loyal to your audience. No matter how far they live from you, remember the world is round, and you might need them in the future.

44) Do not use "Free' in your subject lines since this could arouse suspicion.

Avoid using "Free" in your subject lines. Most people would not mind buying a product or service that is worthwhile. Therefore, do not try to give the impression that you are Santa Claus and only interested in giving out free things. This can arouse suspicion and frighten potential customers.

45) Make your newsletters useful/relevant.

When you use your newsletter as a bait to get contact information, make sure it contains relevant and useful content. Sending your subscribers trash can make them unsubscribe faster than you know it. Worse still, they might choose to mark your newsletter as spam and relegate it to the spam folder for months or even years.

46) Offer freebies to your audience.

You can occasionally offer freebies to your audience. People love free things. You can do this by giving them a link to enable them to download free software, games or even movies. This can motivate them to look forward to receiving your next email. Be unpredictable and keep them guessing which freebies you will offer next.

47) Be on the lookout for new ways to increase subscribers.

Often do research for new ways to increase your subscribers. This is because more and more people are using the same methods to attract subscribers. Therefore, be a step ahead by always improvising new ways that would make and keep you ahead of your competitors. Proper research and innovations on your part can see you go a long way to achieve this objective.

48) Study your competitors and find out what they do differently.

It would be wise to subscribe to the email list of your competitors, especially those who have a high audience-to-customer conversion rate, to see what techniques they use in their emails that enable them to be so successful. Tweak your messages and make them similar to theirs to see whether this would affect the conversion rate.

49) Automate post purchase campaigns.

Set in place automated messages that you can send to your customers after they have made a purchase. This can encourage them to buy more of your products. It is also a good way of interacting with them and ensuring that they do not forget about you.

50) Keep your list current, since email addresses change frequently.

Make sure you periodically ask your subscribers to give you their current email addresses and update your records accordingly. This is because email addresses can change frequently. You should contact people who do not respond to your emails for a long time to see whether they have changed their email addresses.

51) Have a concise privacy policy in place.

Put a privacy policy in place that guarantees all the personal information your customers give you is confidential. Avoid exchanging this information with other email marketers, since that is a serious violation of subscribers' privacy.

52) Make your emails short when they get too frequent.

The more frequent your emails are, the shorter they should become. Include only content that is valuable and which will encourage your readers to take action and buy your products or services. A short message enables a subscriber to save time, especially when it is concise and to the point.

53) Minimize italics and all caps.

Using italics and all caps can look cool, especially when you need to emphasize a point. Nonetheless, remember an email message is not a web page or printed copy. Therefore, minimize on this and allow your content to flow naturally. Make your text readable in all email providers.

54) Experiment with different subject lines.

Keep on experimenting with different subject lines until you find those that are most effective. You should keep a record of all the subject lines you have used in the past and evaluate which are the best. You can make the subject lines more relevant by synchronizing them with the season. For instance, when it is during the Christmas holiday, include that in your subject lines and show your readers why your services or products are important during that season.

55) Respect email as a marketing medium.

Email is an effective marketing medium and you should not use it for selfish gains. This includes gathering emails and selling them at a profit. Remember, the people who are signing up to your email list need the services or products that you offer, and would hate to be bombarded by emails from strangers.

56) Measure results periodically to see what works best for you.

Measure the results of your email campaigns to see what works best for you. Do not be afraid to ask an expert for advice in case you notice you are not making any headway. An expert can point out where you are going wrong and save you valuable time of experimenting.

57) Have a text version of your messages ready at all times.

Although HTML and rich media posts that include video, audio, and animation, can generate more reaction rates, consider having a text version in your media campaigns. The idea is to get relevant subscribers and convert them to customers, not to impress readers with wonderful pictures that might not lead to conversion.

58) Tweak your subject lines after each campaign.

Tweak your subject lines after every email campaign. This will make your messages seem fresh. However, ensure all your messages are an interesting read.

59) Avoid using foul language in your text, no matter how frustrated you may feel with your subscribers.

The usage of foul language in email marketing can be counterproductive. Although some subscribers might send you rude messages at times, especially when you fail to honor your promise to supply them with whatever they needed, or when your services fall below their expectations, hold your horses, and be kind and polite when you respond, no matter how frustrating their accusations might be.

60) Make it easy for your clients to reach you by providing a reliable alternative email address.

As the number of subscribers increases, you will notice that the number of queries increase too. Consider giving your subscribers alternative email address where they can reach you quickly when they need to do that, especially after they have been trying to reach you in vain. Moreover, giving out several different email addresses can make your work easier, since you will not have all your emails cluttered in one inbox.

61) Be punctual in replying to texts and responding to new queries.

Most people do not like to wait for ages for a reply. This can make them lose interest. Put a mechanism in place that can enable you to sort out queries, and reply to them on time. You can set out several days in a week to reply to all queries. Alternatively, you can get an assistant to do that for you.

62) Keep a record of subscribers and those who unsubscribe.

Keeping the record of those who unsubscribe is as important as keeping that of subscribers. Try to find out why people unsubscribe from your email list, especially when there is mass unsubscribes. Probably your emails are poorly written, and you need to tweak them a bit.

63) Give new services and special offers.

Do not stick with selling the same services and products once you get going and have gathered a long email list. That is your chance to expand. Consider offering new services and products to your subscribers so that you can reach as many people on your email list as possible. Remember, different people have different tastes and preferences. What appeals to some might not appeal to others.

Part 3

How to Write Effective Subject Lines

Short, concise and descriptive subject lines are quite effective and trigger the most open rates in the industry because they explain in brief what exactly is in the email. Most people ignore emails that have long subject lines and consider opening them to be a waste of time. You can do a number of things to ensure that your subject lines stand out and tempt the reader to open the email.

- Avoid tasteless or flashy messages, since many subscribers ignore such emails and do not even bother to open them.
- Personalize the message by including the first name of the recipient or the city where they live. Including the city's name has more open rate success, since it shows that you have made the effort to know where your recipient live.
- Avoid commonly used words such as "free" or "you have won" in the subject line. Such words can trigger the spam filters and make your emails to land in the spam folder rather than the inbox.
- Try to be humorous and loose when writing your message. Do not write as if you are writing for a robot. The people who receive your emails are human, and they like to be treated as such. Talk to your readers as real people and not merely potential customers.
- Customize subject line after every email campaign to see which version gets the most open rate. You can do this by segmenting your subscribers by their preference, demographics and taste, and then post a particular message to a small group of people first. Assuming you have 4000 subscribers, send the message to 500 people first to see whether your subject line is catchy. Measure their open rate then modify the subject line accordingly before sending emails to the rest of the group.
- Have a number of subject lines handy at all times. This will enable you to change your subject lines frequently and keep them fresh.
- Avoids all caps, semicolons, exclamation marks, and any other fancy styles, and be straight forward in the subject lines.
- Test subject lines with A/B testing. Create multiple versions of the test version to see which works the best. A/B testing (bucket tests) or split-run testing is simply a term used for randomized experiment that involves two or more variants to see which versions works the best.
- Avoid giving your readers false promises. This might initially increase the number of open emails, but it could compromise your credibility and eventually trigger mass unsubscribes.
- Urge your readers to take immediate action when they receive your email. Give a sense of urgency. This will encourage the readers to act immediately and not delay opening the email until another time.

- Avoid boring details that would not add value to the email. Instead of saying something like, "I am very happy that you are about to open this great email which will instantly change your life," just say, "thanks for taking the time to read this email."
- Phrase your subject line as a question. For instance, "would you like the best email marketing software in town?" Instead of, "I am hereby bringing you the best marketing software in town."
- Make your reader feel special. You can do this by phrasing the subject line in a personal way. Give the impression that the recipient is one of the chosen few.
- Avoid misleading subject lines and do not put subject lines that contain information that is irrelevant to the email. For instance, do not say that you are seeking donations then go ahead to sell a brand to the reader. Make the purpose of the email clear.
- Use "you" voice in the subject line so that it seems you are addressing the recipient directly.

Adding preview text to email could see your open rate shoot up substantially. This enables the subscriber to glimpse the email through the preview panel before they can open it.

Part 4

Email Gathering Options

You can boost sales, increase blog and web traffic, build brand awareness, generate leads, and strengthen relationships, by having permission-based email or opt-in email mechanism in place. Avoid gathering email addresses at random, from friends or social media, and bombarding people with unsolicited emails. Always ensure that you use proper channels to gather and grow your email list, since this could significantly increase your chances of selling your products and services easily. Below are several ways of gathering emails.

Opt-in email

This is the term used when you give the reader the option of receiving email. The success rate of this feature is higher than that of unsolicited bulk email, also known as spam, since the recipient might value your correspondence more when they choose to receive such emails. Opt-in email gathering comes in various forms.

Single opt-in/unconfirmed email

In single opt-in/unconfirmed email, a person subscribes to a mailing list and start receiving emails from the sender. However, the sender does not make an effort to confirm that the email address provided actually belongs to the person who signed up through the email software in their web page or blog, but only sends an email to the recipient, informing them that they will start to receive emails from them shortly.

Double opt-in/confirmed email

With double opt-in/confirmed email, the sender sends the person who signed up to the mailing list a link and asks them to click on it. Failure to click on the link could mean that the recipient has not given the sender permission to send more emails. The sender sends the link so that they can confirm that the person actually signed up to the mailing list. Double opt-in/confirmed email is important because the sender verifies that a third party or malicious person did not sign up using the name of the person who receives the verification email. Thus, they only send further emails to persons who have indicated that they will be interested in further correspondence.

There are two types of emails

 A.) Direct e-mails
 B.)Transactional emails

Direct e-mails

Direct emails are those that the sender sends to introduce their services to the recipient. The services can be the announcement of a catalogue of products, newsletter, soliciting a donation, or promotional material.

Transactional email

The sender typically sends transactional email to trigger an action. They might send it due to an action the recipient took, an action that the recipient was the target, or point out inaction on their part. The user could have been in the process of purchasing a product or promised to do that. The sender therefore sends them this sort of email to confirm the purchase, urge them to complete a transaction, confirm email address, reset password, thank them, give them updates, or ask them to send payment or order more products. The term merely means any email sent to a recipient with the intention of bonding with them, or giving them an interaction with the sender when they sign up in their website. This makes transactional emails to have the highest open rates in the industry. The open rates of these emails are higher than that of commercial emails because the recipient expects them due to an action they took directly. They may have signed up to a service, placed an order, or requested more information about a particular service. Transactional emails are some of the most valuable emails in the inbox of many subscribers.

Transactional Emails versus Commercial Emails

- High deliverability rates as compared to newsletters. This is because they are more highly regarded by the recipient, since they have been expecting them. Moreover, internet service providers do not often mistake transactional emails for spam or send them to the spam folder, as they do with newsletters.
- Since they are action based, the recipient knows that they contain some instructions, and they are more likely to obey these instructions, such as to click a certain link, or send the merchant further instructions about their order.
- They captivate the audience because they signed up for an email list and knew what exactly to expect. Thus, they are willing to respond to them as quickly as possible.
- They bring anticipation since the recipient is waiting for them. Depending on why they signed up to the mailing list, they might be ready to make purchases quickly, since they know the products or services on offer could add value to them.

Return on Investment (ROI) Definition

Return on investment is the computing of the gain earned in each investment in relation to the investment cost. Since we express the result as a ratio or a percentage, it is easy to measure a variety of investments against one another using ROI. Calculating email marketing ROI is important because it enables you to know whether you are making any gains in your marketing campaign, so that you can make informed marketing decisions.

How to Calculate ROI

Calculating ROI is easy. You take the profit you got from an investment (which refers to the income obtained from the sale of an investment), deduct the cost of the investment, and then divide the total by the cost of the investment.

Thus ROI= (Gains-Cost) /Cost.

For example, if you buy 100 pieces of chocolate bars at $5 each, your investment cost would be $500. Suppose you sell the chocolate bars for $750, your ROI would then be ($750-500) /500 making a total of 0.5 or 50%. To confirm this, you take $500 and multiply it by 1.5 to get $750.

Part 5

Email service providers

Although email marketing is among the most effective ways to generate sales for any product, it can be frustrating when you do not know how to go about it. In case you are unsure on how to carry out your email campaign, you can enlist the services of an Email Service Provider (ESP).

Email Service Providers (ESPs) are companies that host email-marketing services on their servers and sent emails to subscribers. Typically, when you sign up for email providing services, you get an email marketing account with a customized web browser interface from where you can send email messages to your subscribers. Email service providers offer several services.

- They provide features that enable you to track the emails you send, delivery success rates, open-rates and click-through rates. You also get to know who among your subscribers opened your messages or clicked the links on them. This enables you to gauge the effectiveness of your email marketing campaign.
- They provide features that enable you to create templates, or utilize pre-made email templates, and test them for compatibility with email applications, including mobile devices.
- They provide attributes that improve delivery rate (AKA Multi-part Mime) by sending both plain and HTML content.
- They incorporate spam-testing features that identify and eliminate factors that place the template at the risk of being blocked by major internet service providers (ISPs). This ensures most of the emails you send out through these services reach the inbox of the recipient. Moreover, they make it possible for you to send bulk emails, which would otherwise not be possible if you use regular internet service providers (ISPs), since they can block bulk emails as spam.
- They provide the ability to customize content so that it is relevant and personalized. This enables you to target specific people in your email marketing campaign who are likely to be interested in your products or content.
- They offer list-segmenting features that enable you to categorize your subscribers according to their preference, demographics, taste etc.
- They have the A/B testing ability to enable you find out which version of your emails works best.
- They provide user-friendly reports that analyze statistics concerning delivery success rates, open-rates and click-through rates (CTR).

ESP policies (acceptable use policy) often referred to as terms and conditions prevent users from sending spam through their systems. This improves delivery rate and minimizes the chances of emails being blocked as spam. An ESP should also automatically include an unsubscribe link in every email you send through their service.

This is because many people get frustrated when they are unable to unsubscribe from an email service. What they end up doing is flagging such emails as spam. When people repeatedly do this, mainstream email providers can flag your emails as spam, leading to the emails you send ending up in the spam folder instead of the inbox. Unlike ESPs, major ISPs do not provide prohibitive bulk email sending functionalities, and that increases the chance of such emails being regarded as spam.

What to look for when selecting an ESP

- Delivery Rate: You should check whether your email service provider has the capacity to ensure all the emails you send are delivered on time. Your ESP should have multiple servers at their disposal, and high speed internet connection, so that when one server is down, they can utilize the other servers. This is important because you will have to insert links that lead to your landing pages, or a catalogue of products, and request a reader to click these links to access your landing pages. Imagine what can happen if your ESP's servers are down and your subscribers are unable to click the links. Many ESPs provide click-tracking tools that redirect clickable links to go through their server then your website so that they can track the click-through rate (CTR).
- Fee structure: Evaluate whether the pricing plan of your email service provider is cost effective. In case you are starting out, go for the free trials. Many ESPs offer a free trial, and you can use this to gauge whether their services suit your needs.
- Mobile optimizing features: Find out whether they optimize their services for mobile devices and make mobile marketing a priority. With everyone being on the go, most people read their emails on their phones. Therefore, you should find out whether they have templates that enable your content to be sharp, even on the mobile, for maximum effect. In addition, they should have a variety of templates from which you can choose. Nonetheless, having a variety of stunning customized templates will not help much if they are not easy to use. Ensure your ESP offer drag-and-drop templates, since they offer the best user experience, and make it quite easy for you to add text and images to your email.
- Your ESP should offer a feature that enables you to do A/B testing (split testing). This involves testing, which method works best for you, by analyzing your subject lines, content, response rate, then segmenting customers by their location, taste and other criteria, comparing results, and determining the best way to leverage your email marketing campaign. You can also use Google analytics to measure the effectiveness of your email campaign.
- Ensure you do not sign up for a service that requires more than one month obligation. Thus, you can opt out easily if the services they offer do not meet your expectations.
- Your ESP should give you a valid private IP address or a shared one with very few users. The sharing of an IP address would mean that when another customer repeatedly sends spam, leading to many spam objections, your internet service provider could blacklist and eventually block the IP address, which could mean your emails would not reach your subscribers. This can negatively affect your email marketing campaign. Sharing an IP address is like sharing a phone number with a

large group of people, which could be counterproductive. Ensure you get your own IP address from your ESP.

- Choose an ESP who enables the integration of your email marketing campaign with social media marketing. Such an ESP should make it easy for you to share your emails on social media, be it promotional or advertising content, so that you can reach a maximum number of people.
- Your ESP should provide regular training on email marketing best practices online or through the phone. This can enable you to understand the basic concept behind email marketing and how best to implement it. Such training will enable you to launch an effective email marketing campaign in the future without having to depend on ESPs.
- Your ESP should ensure that emails are not delayed when subscribers send bulk emails at the same time.
- They should provide the appropriate setting that you can tweak to ensure that ISPs do not consider your emails as spam when you send them out in bulk form.
- They should have been in the game for long and have a good reputation with ISPs, who have verified that they do not send spam through their systems.
- At one time or another, you will discover that you need a helping hand in your email marketing campaign. Your ESP should have a supportive customer care to assist you in your efforts.
- People no longer only read emails on computers, but many internet-enabled phones now access emails too. Ensure your ESP provides the functionality to enhance brand for mobile applications and offer the user a nice experience while interacting with your brand. You can also optimize acquisition forms for mobile, which a person can fill out using their Smartphone or tablet. Many users ignore or delete emails that are not optimized for mobile. Also, do not leave out people who have no Smartphone or tablets. Make your emails, optimized for all phone models. You should also be aware of how your emails are displayed in different mobile devices such as touchscreens and how you can optimize their appearance to give your reader the best user experience.
- Your ESP should have the ability to use social media to spread word about your brand. They should also have features that enable people to like, share or re-tweet your brand details through social media.
- They should have the capacity to track abandoned carts and minimize such incidents.
- Ensure your ESP can track how often your current customers purchase your brand, and follow that up by sending them relevant messages about the brand, when the time comes for them to make another purchase, whether it is in a week, a month, or in a year.
- They should offer features that suppress those who are trying to unsubscribe.
- They should make it easy for you to comply with CAN SPAM act regulations by automatically, including an unsubscribe link to all the emails you send through their service, and remove such emails from your list.
- They should encourage you to send content only to subscribers who have opted-in to receive emails.
- They must be able to plan your email campaign in a professional organized manner, which is cost effective. Moreover, they should have good pricing plans. Many ESPs typically charge a monthly fee based on the number of email addresses on your list or

the maximum number of emails you expect to send. Their fee structure should suit your pockets.

Features To Look For In Bulk Email Software

Bulk email software, also known as mass mailer, usually legitimately sends emails to email list subscribers using direct send and SMTP server. The large numbers of emails sent during spam campaigns make it impossible for spammers to use bulk email software.

Here are some common features to look out for when determining the best bulk email software.

- Free image hosting
- List segmenting features
- Opt-in email forms
- It should have subscriber list management features, which enables contact management, since it includes sign-up and unsubscribing features.
- Built-in templates
- Autoresponders
- New template creation editor facilitated by drag-and drop functionalities
- Reports of deliverability statistics, open ratio and click-through ratio
- Split-testing features

Third party companies usually host bulk-email software programs and sell customers the access to these systems. Get Response, Aweber, Atomic Email Service, Campaign Monitor, Constant Contact and Mailchimp are a good example of such companies.

About the Author

John Griffiths is a freelance writer who has written numerous articles that are all over the internet. He mostly writes on health, fashion, marriage and relationships, and the environment, among other topics.

Contents

www.ingramcontent.com/pod-product-compliance
Lightning Source LLC
Chambersburg PA
CBHW071601170526
45166CB00004B/1753